HOW TO DISAPPEAR FROM THE INTERNET COMPLETELY WHILE LEAVING FALSE TRAILS

HOW TO BE ANONYMOUS ONLINE

By

Raymond

Phillips

Published by:

CSB Academy Publishing Company.

P.O. Box 966

Semmes, Alabama 36575

Cover & Interior designed

By

Carrie Wilson

First Edition

TABLE OF CONTENTS

WIPE YOURSELF OFF THE ONLINE GRID

There are lots of reasons to disappear and go off the grid. This means getting away from the entire digital world. Maybe you are tired of all the digital ads that come your way every day whether it is at your work email or through your social network sites. Perhaps you simply want to get away from things for awhile or perhaps you want to disappear and start a new life. Either way, you will need to completely wipe yourself off the online grid.

Your reasons for going off the grid are your own. However, as you've likely learned; it won't be easy. Search for your name on the internet, and you will be surprised to see how easy you are to find. Computer IP addresses can be tracked, and this is where your problems start. Cell phones, credit card purchases, travel check-ins and even just a toll booth can trace you. Even individuals can simply search for your digital footprint and track where you are.

If you truly want to disappear and start a new life, you are going to have to be prepared to go at it alone. Whether on the run or just settling down to a less digital life, there are a few things you need to do.

LOSE YOUR CELL PHONE

A cell phone is a digital bull's eye that allows people to easily triangulate your position based on your cell signal. You don't even need to make a call to be tracked due to their built-in GPS.

You can remove the battery in order to protect yourself when not using your phone. Replace the battery for a true emergency when you have to use your cell phone. You can also go on the run without a cell phone and leave you're somewhere for people to use, so it misdirects those trying to find you. You definitely don't want to get a cell phone that is difficult to access the battery.

This doesn't mean you have to go entirely without a cell phone. You can easily and cheaply purchase prepaid phones at department stores or gas stations. You can give one to someone you want to keep in contact with and keep the other for yourself. You can even purchase one without having to show an ID.

For extra protection, don't use your phone to make a direct phone call. Rather use a prepaid calling card. You can also get some portable, solar-powered chargers for your gadgets, so you don't have to rely on power outlets.

USE GIFT CARDS FOR PURCHASES

You can still make online purchases even if you are disappearing and starting a new life. Use your cash to purchase a credit card gift card like Visa or American Express. You can get these anywhere and then use them to purchase things online and throw away when you are done. The transactions with these cards are between retailers and credit card companies and your personal details aren't required, and nothing will show up on a statement.

DON'T BE SOCIAL

You will definitely have to give up on Facebook and Twitter. It is best just to walk away if you can. If not, then you will need to create anonymous accounts from a remote location. You should definitely not friend or follow anyone you actually know.

ERASE INFO ASSOCIATED WITH PICTURES

If you are in the habit of sending or posting digital pictures, you should at the very least remove the EXIF data that comes with the image file. This information can include the make of the camera, date and time the picture was taken and in the case of some modern cameras; geographical location information. With enough pictures and time, people can easily find a pattern and know where you've been and where you're likely to be going.

ENCRYPT MESSAGES

You may still need to send emails on occasion. Obviously, you are going to need to set up a new account. Even then you still want to make sure no one can read what you send. It is a good idea to use Gmail from Google since they default to using SSL encryption when you're on their website. This will help if you are using public Wi-Fi.

For added security, you want to encrypt any messages you send. There is a number of free open-source software that can help you with encrypting your messages.

HIDE YOUR IP ADDRESS

The most definite way to be noticed is to visit websites that collect IP addresses from visitors. This can even be the case with some Facebook applications. After an IP address is matched to your PC or phone's IP address, it becomes easier for law enforcement or clever hackers to call the ISP assigned to the IP address and match it to a user. If you are surfing from a school or business, then you can even be tracked to your specific dorm or cubicle.

A proxy server can be helpful. Tor or The Onion Router will help prevent people from seeing you by re-routing your web page requests through multiple routers on the internet. While people on the other end will see an IP address for a router, it won't be anywhere near your computer. Tor offers bundles for any major operating system and even some smartphones. The bundles can run from USB flash drives, so you don't even need to use your own computer.

DON'T SIGN IN

When it comes to using free Wi-Fi, you will be asked to sign in and create an account. If possible, you want to avoid these places. On the other hand, Starbucks and Barnes and Nobles have an

AT&T Wi-Fi that doesn't require anything more than clicking to re-access every couple of hours. However, once you get online, you can put a VPN to work to help prevent wireless snoopers from seeing what you are looking at.

DON'T LOOK FOR A TAIL

Don't waste your time searching for a digital tail. This is a classic tactic for people tracking you since anyone who is on the run wants to know how close people are to finding them. If you start going online to see what people know about you, your are likely to stumble upon a trap that will announce your location to the people that are looking for you. Avoid Googling yourself or posting misinformation anonymously.

DISAPPEAR AND DECEIVE

Most of the information people find online about you comes from you. Therefore, an easy tactic is to hide in plain sight by filling the internet with incorrect information. This means you can use social networks and other such sites to put out misinformation. While it is important to reduce your digital footprint, you still want to stay online. Use it as a means to deceive people about where you live, your income and members of your family. This will make it harder for pursuers to find you. Consider creating an imaginary life and then start making status updates about it. The more misinformation a pursuer gets, the more time they'll spend going in the wrong direction.

This may seem like a lot of overkill, but it does show you how easily you can be tracked in today's online world. Use common sense when online and don't overshare information. Take appropriate precautions and limit what you put online. We'll discuss some these areas in more detail later.

Whether you are disappearing and starting a new life or you simply want to get away from it all and make your life simpler; disappearing from the internet is something many are choosing to do to protect their privacy.

Anyone who has used the internet has an online identity. This online presence can be very slight: just an email account or a comment on a new site. On the other hand, you might be very prolific on the internet with a number of usernames, accounts, message, and profiles through a number of sites. If you are very active on the internet, you might be able to self-Google your name and what you find can be both enlightening and worrying at the same time.

You shouldn't just worry about your online identity, but also how much information is publicly available. The largest sites on the Internet are driven by online advertising, and their fuel is your personal and alleged private data. Most individuals are fine with privacy trade-offs and the lack of control. However, if you want to get away from this situation and regain control of your privacy, then you need to disappear from the internet. This requires a bit more work than just logging out and deleting accounts, consider how you can disappear from the internet.

When a website first gets started, they don't place much attention and focus on how to help their users leave. However, larger websites such as Facebook, Google, Amazon, and Microsoft have had time to fine-tune their websites and offer users well-defined escape plans; even if these are well-hidden.

If you've ever used any type of Google service, then you likely have a Google account. Google accounts contain quite a bit of personal data. You can type in google.com/dashboard just to get an idea of how much personal information is contained in your Google account. However, it is quite easy to remove this data.

Before you do disconnect, you want to make sure you back up any information that you might want to keep. You have a few months after deletion to recover your Google account in case you change your mind for any reason. While Google doesn't have a software tool for exporting data, most services do have their own that are usually found under the settings menu on the upper right-hand side of the screen.

The easiest way to back up your messages is to add your account to a mail app such as Outlook or Apple's Mail before you delete, this will allow you to backup your contacts as well. After copying your important data offline, you can go to your Google account dashboard at google.com/accounts. Go to My Products and then Edit. Select Close Account and Delete All Service and Info

Associated With It. There will be a list of Google services that you have used. Check the box next to each, along with the two double check boxes at the bottom and then select Delete Google Account. Your accounts will be instantly wiped from the public internet. However, as the warning on the website says it can take up to 60 days for residual information to be deleted from active servers and may remain in backup systems.

Until 2008, there was no specific way to permanently delete all of your information from Facebook. Rather there was a Deactivate option, which took your profile out of public view but left it on Facebook servers indefinitely. When thousands of people started complaining, Facebook built a tool to permanently and instantly delete user data. It is hidden away in the site's Help section.

In order to access it, go to facebook.com/help and type in delete my account in the search box. The top result will take you to the deletion page. Click Submit and confirm your choice and you'll be all done. While Facebook doesn't offer many options when it comes to backing up your data, there are a number of free Facebook apps that can archive your photo albums.

For Microsoft's services, go to account.live.com and scroll down to the bottom. Under the Other Options header, you can click Close Account. You will be taken to a page where you need to re-enter your account password and click 'Yes'. However, there is no account-wide export option.

Closing your Amazon account is a little more difficult. Click Help in the upper right-hand corner on any amazon.com page and search for closing your account. On the results page, pick Contact Us, then click on Something Else. Below this you can select Account Setting from the menu and then Close My Account. At the bottom of the page, you click on the Send Us an Email link, fill out the form that appears and send.

SMALLER WEBSITES

Nearly all websites will offer some type of account deletion option. However, smaller sites that have posted or reposted your data without your permission will be a little more difficult to delete. This is because the owners never had the permission in the first place to republish your blog posts, photos or videos. Finding this information or any comments about you is more difficult than doing a simple search on Google or Bing. Be sure to place quotation marks around your name when searching.

Searching for yourself isn't narcissism; but it is a common practice for job recruiters, current employers or even potential dates to check out a person. A misleading search result or bad information can cause serious issues and damage to your reputation. If you are on the run and trying to disappear it can also lead people to you and ruin your privacy when you are trying to start a new life.

The best option when dealing with smaller websites is to send a direct request for a webmaster to pull all infringing or upsetting material off the website. If there is no prominent contact information for the website's operator or if you don't get a reply from the listed address or phone number, then you can direct information to the site's administrator by doing a search online at whois.net. Domain owners are required by the Internet Corporation for assigned names and number to have contact information for 'Whois' searches, including a phone number. Hopefully, this will at least get you on the phone with an actual person, or you can get a working email address. Whether this contact information will actually be of help to deleting your account is another matter entirely.

If a website refuses to take down content that rightfully belongs to you, you can send a takedown notice. Under the Digital Millennium Copyright Act or DMCA, you have the right to have infringing content such as images, text or video that you rightfully own to be taken off the website. There are multiple forms online for you to submit DMCA notices to internet hosting companies. You can even fill out a form to ask Google, Yahoo, and Bing to remove content from their search results. While these forms won't guarantee a website will work with you, but if you are persistent, you will see good results and sometimes the threat of legal action is going to be enough to get the attention of a website owner. If you still aren't getting results, then it may be time to consider talking to a lawyer.

GETTING RID OF ALL DATA FROM THE WEB

You can easily tell when your data has been removed from public display since you won't be able to find it anymore. However, it can be nearly impossible to find out whether or not a company is still privately holding your data or giving it to third parties. In addition to having no way to verify that all your information is permanently deleted, there also isn't any law or regulation that governs data retention. There is also some data that you can't reclaim; once you click the Submit button, you will be relinquishing control. This is after you've clicked past the 50-page license agreement that most don't take the time to read.

This is an important lesson to learn. While it won't help you to gain full control of your online identity, it does provide you with some valuable information. Once you sign up for an internet service, you want to make sure you trust the parent company and understand the data rights you are giving up. For example, when signing up with Google or Facebook, you are literally selling yourself.

CHOOSING ONLINE PRIVACY TOOLS

There are three tools you can use to help you get more privacy online:

1. PRIVATE BROWSING

Most new internet browsers contain a feature called private browsing, but it can go by a few different titles: Private Mode, Incognito Mode, and InPrivate. All of these names are a bit of an overreach since this mode only prevents web browsers from collecting history and cookies. Basically, it prevents other users of the computer from seeing what you've been browsing, but it won't shield your IP address or existing cookies from any external site.

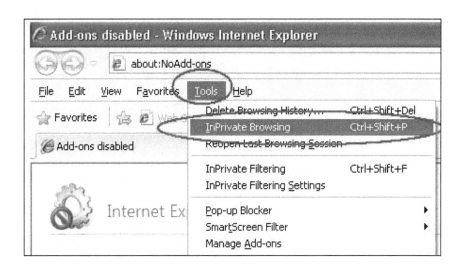

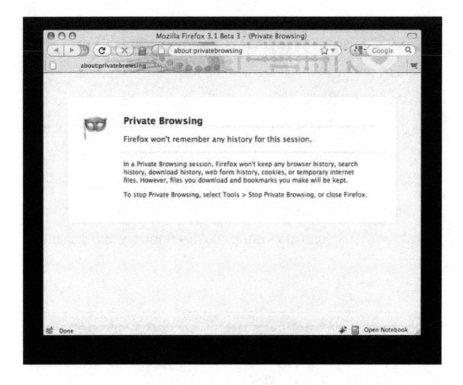

2. VIRTUAL PRIVATE NETWORKS

A paid virtual private network (VPN) service will route your internet traffic through an intermediary in order to mask your computer's address from any site you visit. However, sites will still be able to deposit tracking cookies onto your computer, and your browser is still prone to viruses and exploits. VPNs will reroute all internet traffic, not just from web browsers, but from all sources which is why they are popular with sensitive file sharing communities

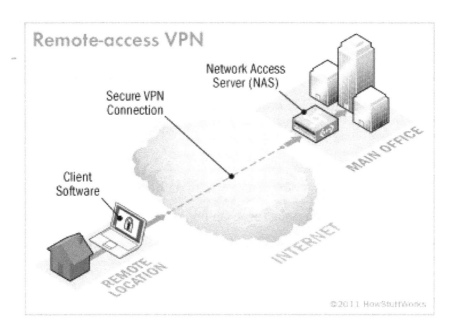

Remote-access VPN

Network Access
Server (NAS)

Secure VPN
Connection

Client
Software

MAIN OFFICE

REMOTE
LOCATION

INTERNET

©2011 HowStuffWorks

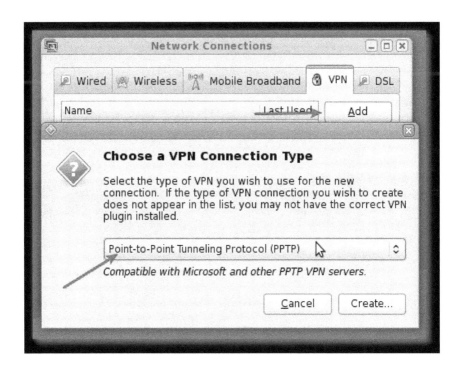

Network Connections

Wired   Wireless   Mobile Broadband   VPN   DSL

Name   Last Used   Add

Choose a VPN Connection Type

Select the type of VPN you wish to use for the new
connection. If the type of VPN connection you wish to create
does not appear in the list, you may not have the correct VPN
plugin installed.

Point-to-Point Tunneling Protocol (PPTP)

Compatible with Microsoft and other PPTP VPN servers.

Cancel   Create...

3. COCOON

This is a plug-in service for the free Firefox browser that combines the advantages of private browsing and a VPN with a few extra security features. Traffic is routed through a remote server and made anonymous. Incoming files from websites or downloads are scanned for malware and viruses. Additional features it offers are throwaway email addresses for spam prevention and full portability so you can access the account from any computer. This makes it a great program for those who are trying to disappear and leave no traces behind for people to follow.

NINE STEPS TO DISAPPEAR FROM THE INTERNET

The following nine steps can help you to disappear from the internet and then once you've created your new identity can help you to anonymously surf the internet. Even if you aren't choosing to disappear, you may want to reduce your social media footprint and your online presence after hearing about all the reports of stolen information as a result of social media.

After completing the nine steps below you will be able to deactivate your accounts, remove links to yourself from search results and remove yourself from lists so you can stay hidden online. If you really want to disappear, there will also be some tips on how you can use the internet anonymously.

1. DEACTIVATION

The first step you need to take is to deactivate all your online social media accounts. This includes both larger sites like Facebook, Twitter, and Google as well as any smaller websites you may be a part of. Refer to the above steps to help you close out your accounts on these websites.

2. SEARCH FOR YOURSELF

The second step is to search for yourself online. This will help you find the websites you may have signed up for a long time ago, but since forgotten about. For example, a MySpace account you opened when it was first popular; but have since stopped using due to your more active Facebook account.

3. LEAVING FALSE TRAILS

There are going to be certain accounts and websites where information can't be deleted. If this is the case, then you should at least change the information to false information such as fake names and locations. This way if someone does access these accounts they won't be able to track your location. You can even use it to develop a false trail and send those looking for you in the opposite direction.

4. UNSUBSCRIBE FROM MAILING LISTS

In step four, you want to unsubscribe from any mailing lists you signed up for with your email. You can look to your email inbox and junk folder for a good starting point.

5. DELETE SEARCH ENGINE RESULTS

While searching for your name on Google you will find a number of links that include information about you. Contact the major search engines and ask for them to be removed. For example, Google has their own URL removal tool. However, most search engines aren't obliged to remove links; especially if the website is owned or hosted by someone other than you. If this is the case, then you need to move on to step six.

Google

Content removal

Help with: Use this page to request removal of a page or site from Google's search
Reincluding content in   results. (Not all requests are successful. Here's why.)
search
Keeping personal
information out of Google
SafeSearch / Adult   **Create a new removal request**
content
Help center   Enter the URL that you'd like to remove (case-sensitive)
Search help   Go   Continue

6. CONTACT WEBSITES TO HAVE DATA REMOVED

If a search engine doesn't remove links that contain information about you, then you will need to contact the websites directly and ask them to remove the references. This process is difficult and can sometimes take awhile so you will want to get this started as soon as possible.

7. DATA CLEARING HOUSES

Unfortunately, there are data collection sites they are also known as data clearing houses or data brokers that collect your personal information. You may ask why they do that. Well, it is a big business, they sell those data to various internet and other marketing agencies who want to send you email or direct mail based on your shopping and other preferences based on your information. Let's say you have a passion for golf, you also play video games and you buy a lot of health and beauty related products from online, once these data companies enter all those data into their system along with your age, gender, and location, their unique algorithm can then come up with some unique products and services that may peak your interest. To some marketers, this information is extremely valuable, and they pay top dollar for it.

As difficult as it is to have individual websites remove your information, the most difficult process is to get a data clearing house to remove your data. Data clearinghouses are companies that collect and sell data to other firms for profit. Often you will need to have persistent phone calls and letters in order to completely have yourself removed from these lists.

Top 3 data brokers:

- Spokeo
- Crunchbase
- PeopleFinder

8. HIDE YOUR PHONE NUMBER

Next, you want to contact phone companies and online directories to ask them to make your phone number, and email addresses unlisted.

9. DELETE ALL EMAIL ACCOUNTS

Lastly, after you have successfully removed yourself from online public areas; you need to take yourself away from the internet. Do this by deleting all your email accounts.

Once you have removed yourself from online, if you want to stay hidden and yet still use the internet you are going to have to be very careful. You will need to learn to master reputation management, learn to use dummy accounts and take advantage of anonymous searches.

While disappearing from the internet isn't for everyone, it can be a good way to free up your life. If you are serious about protecting your privacy, security and reputation then you definitely want to consider making yourself invisible online.

Once you have disappeared from the online world, you need to know how to stay hidden and keep yourself private online. Let's consider how you can do this.

8 STEPS TO STAYING PRIVATE ONLINE

With the recent exposure of the NSA spying scandal continuing to have impacts throughout the world, more people are becoming aware of their lack of privacy online. As a result, more individuals are looking for ways to stay private online to avoid their information from being accessed and utilized.

It isn't true paranoia anymore to think you are being watched. There are number of people/companies watching your every move online. Documents leaked by NSA whistleblower Edward Snowden illustrated this point when it showed the reach of the biggest intelligence agencies. Perhaps the scariest part is knowing that agencies collaborate with technology companies to weaken security tools and make it easier to spy on the general public aka people like me and you.

Whether it is the intelligence community or a third party ad network from Facebook or Google, private information can be accessed online and analyzed to be used by a variety of organizations in ways that are hard to predict. This can be a big deal. If you want to disappear and start a new life, you certainly don't want people to locate you, but even if you just want to live under the radar; it is still difficult to get online when you know people or companies maybe still watching you. Whether it's your email or online banking, you can no longer assume that your data is safe or at the very least that you aren't the only one with access to it.

As a result of this invasion of privacy, many users are starting to look for open-source privacy tools to help them stay anonymous online. These tools are transparent and independently audited so they can't be subverted as easily as other proprietary tools. This is the best way to maintain privacy online to stay under the radar. How exactly can you protect your privacy online? Is it possible to hide your tracks online from everyone trying to gain access to it? Not only is it possible, but it is something the average person can do in a few basic steps. Consider what you can do to stay private online.

1. DO NOT TRACK

The first step that many people take to help themselves feel protected online is to sign up for a 'Do Not Track' feature. This is available on all of the major browsers such as Safari, Chrome and Internet Explorer. The only issue is, they don't really work. Do Not Track is a voluntary standard that most marketers don't follow. A better option is to install the plugin DoNotTrackMe by Abine. This plugin does actually block most third-party ads and works with all the major browsers. Another good plugin is Ghostery, which displays right in your browser all the cookies that track you while you're online.

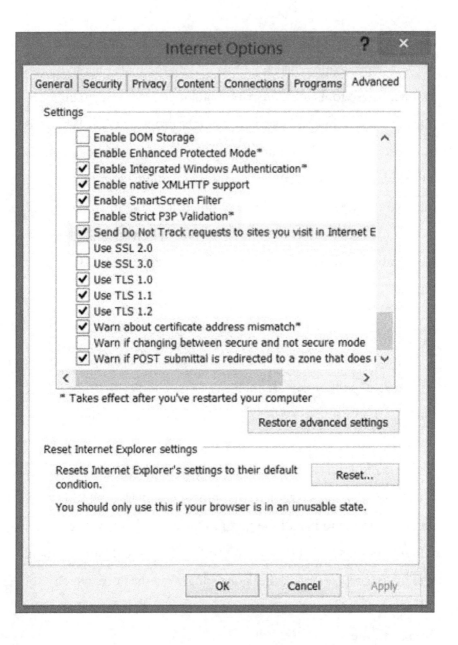

2. CHANGE SEARCH ENGINES

If you want to be hidden while on the internet, then you shouldn't use Google or Bing for your searches. These sites are known for gathering data from user searches, and they store or share that information for third parties to use. Rather it is safer and more secure to use a smaller, private browser such as StartPage or DuckDuckGo.

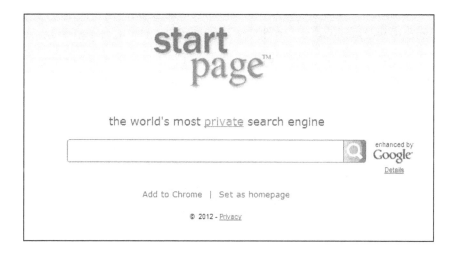

3. DIY EMAIL

A third party email has absolutely no form of privacy. This is something you need to accept if you are going to stay private online. Gmail, Yahoo Mail and Outlook all data mine your email contents and share at least metadata with third party advertisers. All of these emails providers and even more of the privacy-focused ones are also highly susceptible to government requests for access to user data. To stay private online while using the email you need to host your very own mail server that only you can access. However, there are limitations to this option which we will discuss in the next point.

Another option is public key cryptography. At one time, only IT experts could do something known as public key cryptography. Today, more people can use tools like OpenPGP (stands for Pretty Good Privacy) in order to keep communications private such as emails and file transfers.

In simple terms, with a tool like OpenPGP, you will be generating two unique keys. A public key is given to others, and they can use it to encrypt messages they sent to you. A private key is the one you keep secret and safe since it works along with your public key in order to unlock messages sent to you. A public key cannot decrypt a message so you can give it out to anyone you want and not worry about them reading your messages.

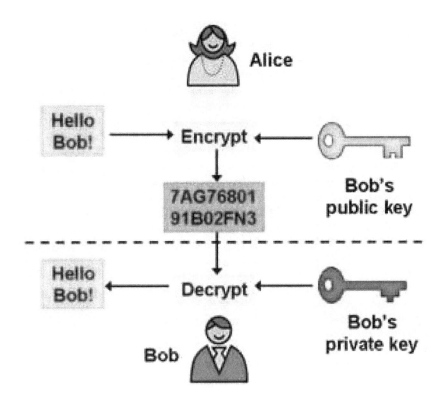

4. ENCRYPTION

From leaked documents, we know that intelligence agencies have collaborated with technology companies to have back doors installed on security products. This means that most proprietary encryption software will likely be compromised. Rather it is safer to use open-sourced programs to encrypt data.

An absolute must if you want to stay private online is to encrypt all your online communications especially email. Even when you host your own mail server, your mail is going to be traveling over the internet and through other people's networks before eventually ending up on another mail server. When you encrypt your email, you will be getting some added protection. This isn't that difficult to do since there are many free services out there that offer this option.

Many of these open-source software programs offer volume, partition and drive encryption; in addition most have the ability to set up hidden volumes or even hide an entire operating system. This means that if you reveal your main encryption password for any reason, the hidden volume will still stay encrypted and undetectable in the visible volume. Basically, it is like having a safe room inside a safe room.

5. SECURE INTERNET TRAFFIC

Don't place all your focus and energy on securing your email and browser settings. You also want to think about your internet traffic in general. Everything you do online is sent through on Internet Service Provider (ISP) to another and in the meanwhile can go through a number of corporate and private servers. To protect your privacy from this, there are two things you need to do. First, you want to use The Onion Router (TOR) to hide your IP address when browsing online or sending messages. Second, you want to use total encryption to hide the actual content of your traffic by using a virtual private network (VPN).

Tor is a popular free and open virtual network that bounces communications throughout the world in order to prevent sites from learning your physical location. Tor is used as the basis for a range of security applications. The most common of these applications is the increasingly popular Tor browser. This application is based on a modified Firefox release, so it is easy to use, and if you use a few simple precautions you will be able to have a certain level of anonymity while browsing the internet.

In addition, Tor is easy to use since you only have to download the Tor Browser Bundle and everything you need is included. Once you run the downloaded file, everything will be setup automatically for you. However, you should be aware that browsing with Tor isn't quite the same as browsing with other software since it is stripped of a lot of the modern features.

It should also be noted that Tor browser only protects against traffic that goes through the Tor browser. Tor isn't a VPN client so you can't expect it to protect you from everything. You will also have reduced browsing speeds since data files have to be bounced around the world. So Tor is a great option for those who want to stay hidden online, but not for those who want to use it for everyday use or time sensitive tasks.

6. DELETE STORED DATA

You can go a step further in protecting your privacy by removing any stored data about you from the internet. Data brokers are focused on collecting information about individuals throughout the United States. While you can remove yourself manually from these brokers, the most efficient way to pay for a service that does it for you such as Abine or DeleteMe. They typically cost around $120-$150 per year, and it is a yearly subscription service.

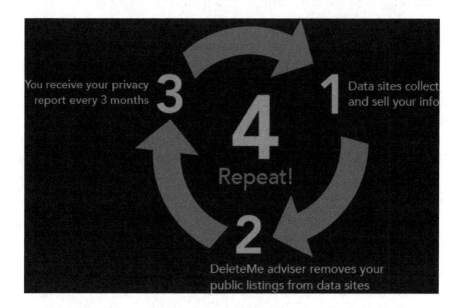

7. SECURE YOUR PHONE

Just because we are discussing online privacy doesn't mean we are limited to the internet and computers. To truly secure your online privacy you also need to make sure you secure your Smartphone. The first step is to make sure you always use a VPN on your phone. You should also use a program like Gliph to encrypt your texts and picture messages. Second, you want to turn off your phone's GPS and disable geotagging on pictures taken from your phone. Lastly, be careful when downloading applications. There are a number of rogue apps that can steal your data and even some legitimate ones that will ask for access to your personal data when they don't really need it. Check out a later chapter in this book for more details on how you can secure your cell phone.

Nearly everyone uses some form of social network these days. Even if you only use it to keep up with family and friends, you are already compromising some form of your privacy. The least you can do is make sure you have selected the highest level of privacy settings available through the social network site and give careful consideration to why type of information you are sharing with the network. For the best privacy, you can consider using smaller networks rather than the larger ones that are linked with third party advertisers.

Using just one or two of these above tactics won't be enough to completely protect your online privacy. If you use all of them together then you will be able to put together a comprehensive strategy that provides you with a high level of protection for your online privacy. One thing that can help you put all of these together in an easy to use option is tails. Let's discuss a little about them.

TAILS

Tails is a program that allows you to have every tool you need in one rather than having individual tools. This live operation system is Debian-based, and you can run it on any PC from a DVD or USB drive since it only uses the host system's RAM and leaves no trace when you switch it off or disconnect. You can use it at any public internet site and not worry about spyware and viruses getting on your operating system. Tails can also be used to circumvent regional locks and internet censorship.

However, the drawbacks to this option is that you need to boot from a disc or external drive so you can run Tails on a PC that has a locked down BIOS that will only boot from an internal hard drive.

Tails includes a range of tools that are pre-configured to connect to the internet through a Tor network. This means it blocks any attempts by other applications to access the internet. When you use the combined tools to maximum effects with Tails, you will be able to be fully anonymous and private online.

Online security doesn't just mean your computer. Let's also take a moment to look at your cell phone's security.

SECURE YOUR CELL PHONE

You may be wondering what a cell phone has to do with disappearing from the internet. In today's modern and electronic world, the cell phone is what keeps many people connected to both the internet and the electronic world as a whole. If you truly want to disappear and live under the radar, then you need to know how to properly secure your cell phone. Unfortunately, most people don't realize the importance of securing a cell phone and therefore make it easier for themselves to be tracked or to lose their personal data.

THE BROAD SPECTRUM OF CELL PHONE SECURITY

There is no one simple solution to all cell phone privacy and security. This is due to the fact that there are too many service providers, too may phone types and too many countries coupled with a lack of fully developed security solutions and not much compatibility between devices. This chapter is going to focus on what information you want to keep private and a few simple ways to do it. Most of this information is directed towards smartphones, but even other phones can be made more secure as well. This chapter helps you to implement your optimum privacy configuration to give you a more secure cell phone.

Laws vary by country. So in some places, it may be illegal to use some of these cell phone security tools or techniques. It is important you investigate the laws in your area before using any techniques that may cause you to violate the law. Violating the law is going to have a much bigger impact on your privacy than simply complying with the law and not securing your cell phone.

SUBSCRIBER INFORMATION

From the moment you buy a phone, your name is attached to it. You are signing a contract with you name on it, and you are making your payments with a credit card that has your name on it. Even if you can avoid these areas of information, you will still do some activities on your phone that will tie the device to you.

When you keep your subscription information private, you will be able to prevent governments from accessing information with and without warrants, subpoenas or due process. It will also protect your cell phone from hackers and rogue employees who compromise networks and databases in order to steal your valuable personal data.

PREPAID CELL PHONES

One option that still exists today is prepaid cell phones that you can buy with cash without having to sign a contract. You can also reload your minutes by paying with cash. Prepaid cells can be used for all communications or just for your most sensitive communications. However, a prepaid phone will still gather enough data at some point after awhile to identify you. So if you choose to use a prepaid cell phone you want to replace them often.

PUBLISHED AND UNLISTED NUMBERS

Nearly any phone number can be found in online directories. Directories are compiled from a vast amount of data that companies across the internet gather from customers. If you give your phone number to a company or even call them; they will record your number in a database. From there it is easy for your phone number to get shared, sold and copied many times by both legal and illegal sources including hackers, governments, corporations, thieve and stalkers.

A phone number may not seem like a big piece of personal data, but it is a major piece of personal data. A phone number will paint a data profile that identifies you and leads to a lot more information about you. Your phone number can easily be used to cause you harm.

The first step you need to take is to ask your service provider to unlist your phone number. Contact the major databases that collect phone numbers such as Intelius and Acxiom. Find out and follow their procedures to help you unlist your phone number. Avoid getting back in these databases by not giving out your number or giving out a fake number to those who don't really need your number. Then there are three other ways you can hide your phone number.

First, there is the option of blocking caller ID. This option is allowed through many carriers. This way, anyone who calls you won't be able to get your phone number. In the United States, you can use *67 to block caller ID before an individual call, but it will cost you.

Second, you can use call forwarding. This option forwards calls from your public number to a private number. Therefore, your private number stays confidential. A good free call forwarding service is Google Voice.

Lastly, you can use a Spoofcard. With this, you can appear to be calling from any number you want while protecting your actual phone number.

PROTECT YOUR LOCATION

Your service provider's cell towers are constantly triangulating your general location through your cell phone. Anyone looking for you can use your precise GPS coordinates and Wi-Fi networks close to you to monitor your activity and even record it. Whenever you use your cell phone, your location is logged.

This data can be accessed by governments, with and without warrants. Thieves can also use this information to target your house when you go on vacation. A hacker can know how to ping your cell phone at any time to determine where it is, even if you aren't actively using your cell phone.

You can turn your cell phone off to make sure you aren't connecting to remote Wi-Fi spots. This can also prevent your general location from being triangulated, and your GPS coordinates from being tracked. This is a general step for basic cell phone security. However, malware can continue to broadcast information on your location even when you turn off your cell phone. This is generally uncommon, but you can prevent this by removing the battery from your phone.

Take a moment to consider the amount of information that is stored on your phone: contact lists, calendars, text messages, photos, call logs, browsing history and more. The most basic part of cell phone security is to secure the phone itself.

Governments that gain access to your phone can use the information to convict you of crimes or learn of your past identity. Competitors can get inside information that can harm a business if employees don't practice good security techniques. Thieves can get vital information such as bank records, passwords and other valuable pieces of personal information that are stored on your cell phone.

Most cell phones today allow you to adjust settings, so you store less history on the actual phone. This can make certain information on your phone less vulnerable such as old text messages, call logs, and other sensitive data.

It is best to lock your phone with a password protection. This not only prevents the embarrassing butt dialing, but it also helps to keep out curious or illegal individuals. However, this still won't protect against thieves and hackers that know how to get around password protection unless you encrypt your phone.

A good manual way of securing your phone is to regularly delete unwanted data. As with your home computer, data isn't truly gone until it is overwritten. However, for casual thieves or those curious about your information it will be enough to stop them.

You wouldn't leave you checkbook or credit cards just lying around for anyone to have access to. The same should be applied to your cell phone. All a person needs is a few minutes alone with your phone in order to install software or hardware that can overcome nearly all cell phone security precautions. If someone you don't trust has had access to your cell phone recently, then you want to think carefully before using it again.

Some phones have a program that allows you to completely wipe the phone memory remotely. If your phone is ever lost or stolen, you can use this to make sure your data isn't compromised. You can also use this option to wipe your phone before you dispose of it.

If you want to make sure all of your data is well protected, then you need full encryption. This will work against everything except the most sophisticated attacks. Open source encryption is best since there is no entity that will provide a back door. There are several open source options available right now so you can easily find one that is easy for you to use.

You can also do partial encryption on your phone. There are several Smartphone apps that allow you to encrypt certain types of data while leaving the rest of your phone unprotected. It can be difficult to make sure there are no copies of data elsewhere on the phone that is only partially encrypted. However, this can be a good option if you only have a few confidential files you want to be encrypted. Again, it is best to go with open source programs, but you can also use trusted encryption software.

PROTECT YOUR CONVERSATIONS

Often if you are going to have a confidential call with a business partner, family member or other individual; no one else is invited to be listening in on the conversation. However, an un-secure cell phone network means governments and illegal individuals can secretly listen in on your conversations. There is also the risk that malicious software can be installed on your cell phone to record conversations. Consider how you can protect your conversations while on your cell phone.

A Voice Over IP (VOIP) is the best option to secure your conversations. Many cell phones allow you to use VOIP to communicate over the internet rather than over a cell phone network that may be compromised. A VOIP app might already be available on your phone, or you can use one through your phone's internet connection. You will still have to trust that the VOIP service is not eavesdropping on your conversation. For this purpose, it is best to use open source VOIP software, but you can use other software if it is trusted. Again, this software still won't protect you against malicious software that is installed on your phone.

While not as common as with computers, cell phones can also be infected with viruses and malware. This is why there are antivirus software programs for cell phones. You won't be able to use the same antivirus software that's on your computer to protect against viruses. You can also reduce your risk of viruses by not opening suspicious email attachments or clicking on questionable links just as you would on a computer. You can also only download apps that you trust or that come from trusted sources.

PROTECTING YOUR TEXTS

Text messages are perhaps the most unsecure feature on your phone. These messages travel through the cell phone network unencrypted and can be stored on your phone for a long time. Text messages are available to anyone who has access to your phone such as governments, hackers, thieves, and competitors. These messages can be accessed by the cell phone network, provider's records, your phone and a number of other ways.

There are a few apps available that can encrypt your text messages while in transit and on your device. There are some web-based IM programs and those specifically designed for cell phones that can encrypt and protect your cell phone security and text communications better than regular text messaging. Again, it is best to trust open source IM software and no a large provider.

PROTECTING VOICEMAIL

Voicemails are stored by your service provider on a server. A number of people can have authorized and unauthorized access to this voicemail information. A few VOIP services will offer encrypted voicemail. However, you still have to trust the VOIP service. For this reason, a small offshore VOIP is less likely to reveal confidential data than larger service providers.

PROTECTING PHOTOS

Smartphones take a lot of photos, how many do you have on your phone right now? In addition to taking a photo, there is also a lot of hidden data in the picture file known as EXIF data. This can include time, date, and GPS coordinates among other information. Any photo that you email or upload from your phone will also export this EXIF information. There are a couple of things you can do to protect against this.

First, you can turn GPS tracking off. Most phones let you turn off geotagging in the settings menu. When you do this, you will prevent data from being added to the picture file.

Second, you can wipe sensitive data before you email or upload your photos. There are several programs that allow you to remove the EXIF data from images. This way you can safely send and share photos without having to share any identifying information.

PROTECT MOBILE APPS

Mobile apps allow you to have a number of neat features and games on your phone. They also provide you with a lot of powerful tools that you can use for business and personal purposes. However, a lot of them also mine a lot of data from your phone that you may not want to share. For example, Linked-In stores your username and password in plain text. Since a lot of people use the same username and password for multiple websites, this can be very damaging if it isn't protected. A lot of other apps do similar things, and a few even have malicious code hidden within them.

The best way to protect yourself is to minimize your usage of apps and only use those from trusted sources that help to increase the security of your cell phone. Before installing an app make sure you research what data they access and use them only if you don't mind sharing information and are sure there is no malware being installed along with them.

PROTECT EMAIL

Email is the modern digital equivalent of a postcard. The message goes through several servers en route to its destination. Along the way, anyone can read it. At the very least your email provider will keep a log of your emails that can be subpoenaed by governments.

You should try to encrypt emails that are sent from your cell phone so that no one can read them during transit. If your recipient is also using encryption, then the message will be completely protected from end to end.

PROTECT WEB BROWSING

An internet provider can view every website you go to, and they can see every wireless network that your cell phone connects to, this is a major breach of privacy. All of this data is readily available to anyone who wants to access it. Most of this data is kept right on your phone where people can easily find it.

Some cell phones allow you to use VPNs like a TOR network. If this is the case, then no one can see where you go on the internet. The VPN records can only be available to governments with court orders.

This is just an outline of the basics that are available to you. There is no cell phone that can offer the complete security of personal information. So you need to figure out what protection you need and make your cell phone as secure as possible.

SOURCE & RESOURCES

To stay up to date on this ever changing world of internet, it is often a good idea to check these sites for the latest information of how to stay safe and hidden on the net.

Here is a great info graphic done by Time Magazine that shows all the steps you need to take, it is a very well thought out info graphics, just take a look at it.

http://time.com/13002/this-infographic-show-how-to-completely-erase-your-identity-from-the-internet/

https://www.cnet.com/how-to/remove-delete-yourself-from-the-internet/

http://www.wikihow.com/Delete-Yourself-from-the-Internet

http://lifehacker.com/5958801/how-to-commit-internet-suicide-and-disappear-from-the-web-forever

Thanks to all these following sites for their beautiful Images

blogspot.no

Bing.com

Google.com

CPSIA information can be obtained
at www.ICGtesting.com
Printed in the USA
LVHW081444010421
683219LV00016B/1150